Long Field Hollow

Praise for *Long Field Hollow*

Marilyn's collection of poems, *Long Field Hollow*, offers a capsule of the beauty, joy, magnificence, and silence that living in a remote mountain oasis affords her and Ellen, to whom this collection is dedicated. It exposes the hardships they have overcome to be part of a mountain community, while, literally and figuratively, building a comfortable environment to foster wellness, security, and peace.

—John King, Black Mountain, North Carolina

Through perhaps all great writing, we, as readers, are given permission to experience, remember, and conjure the stories of our own lives. Marilyn's writing does just that. The depth of her honesty, awareness, love, and humor is truly a gift for all of us who value a strong sense of place and being.

—Tom Dancer, Penland, North Carolina

Marilyn McVicker's *Long Field Hollow* explores the vast panorama that comes along with her intentional move to the mountains. An epigraph from John Milton sets the stage with *"it were an injury . . . against Nature not to go out and see her riches, and partake in her rejoicing."* McVicker invites us to the banquet of life in the Hollow, where *"the silence is grand as any Steinway, the air silky as the finest damask."* Marilyn *"claim[s] this place to stand and love in . . . the words shaking free."* She wrestles with the isolation of the mountains, *"the undulating vapor . . . shrouded in pervasive moisture. Alone in our own cocoons . . . engulfed in my own situation,"* while, like the moth, *"being pulled incessantly towards life. Towards death."* Her honest words challenge us to *"feel [our] soul[s] shudder."*

—Anne Maren-Hogan, Celo, North Carolina,
author of *Vernacular*, winner of NC Poetry Society's
2021 Lena M. Shull Book Contest

Long Field Hollow

poems by Marilyn McVicker

Long Field Publications

Long Field Publications
www.marilynmcvicker.org

ISBN: 979-8-218-18707-1

Cover design and photos: Erin Talbert
Book layout: Celo Book Production Service

To the flora and fauna
who share their resplendent cove with us.

To Ellen.

Remember that very little
is needed to make a happy life.
—Marcus Aurelius, *Meditations*

In those vernal seasons of the year,
when the air is calm and pleasant,
it were an injury and sullenness
against Nature not to go out and see
her riches, and partake in her rejoicing
with heaven and earth.
—John Milton, *Tractate of Education*

Contents

Acknowledgments xi

Preface xiii

Soaring 1
Finer Things 2
Spring Fantasy 3
The Words Shaking Free 4
Chicory 5
Radio Culture Collage 6
Praise Song 7
To Coriander 8
Pas de Deux 9
Coyotes 10
What Kind of Support Does Your Garden Need? 11
Standing in the Fog 12
Dear Subcontractor 14
A Stitch in Time 16
Hot July 18
The Moth 19
Meditation 20
Homecoming 21
The Grandmother Tree Fell 22
Yellow 23
White Cows on a Green Hill 24
Drinking Tea 26
October Full Moon 27

About the Author 29

Acknowledgments

Thanks to the editors who previously published
the following works:

Carolina Mountains Literary Festival Anthology: A Celebration of Ten Festivals,
Press 53, "The Moth," 2015

Gateways, Mayland Community College, "Soaring," 2013

Kakalak, "Standing in the Fog," 2018

Speckled Trout Review, "The Words Shaking Free," 2020

WNC Woman: Women Nurturing Change,
"Coriander," "Pas de Deux," 2012

Preface

At the suggestion of our physician,
we sold our Baltimore house
and moved to the rural mountains.

The land we purchased was known as
"Long Field Hollow."

This is a story of nature and neighbors,
community and connection,
trees, coyotes and contractors.
A story of fear, praise and beauty.
Of hiking, gardening, quilting,
building and drinking tea.
Of hard work and disappointment.
Of solitude and enchantment.

Soaring

No matter what it takes,
I will be free,
as wind
moving through wheat fields and orchards,
across vineyards and oceans,
as unfettered as a gull gliding solo,
leaning into the wind with all her weight,
trusting her own body to carry her onward.

No matter what it takes,
I will be free.
I will know what it is like
to stand alone on the beach,
stretch out my wings,
unruffled by the salt spray,
fling myself onto the wind,
and soar.

Finer Things

I live in the country for medical reasons.
Not for work. Not for family or education.

Not for culture or fine arts. I am here for fresh air
and freedom. I never knew I would live in a place

so remote. Without trash pick-up or a daily
newspaper. I grew up with oriental rugs, fine china,

box seats at the concert hall, piano lessons, Cecchetti
ballet. In my teens I attended cotillion. Learned how to

take a man's arm, dance, make polite conversation.
You would never know it now, as I weed the gravel drive.

Wrangle the pick-up over rocks and ruts. Struggle to keep
the forest back. As we go through tires and firewood

in a life I never planned. But when I stand in the dark,
watch the moon come over the ridge and light up our cove,

the silence is as grand as any Steinway, the air silky
as the finest damask.

Spring Fantasy

I watch from the front porch.
Mid-May. A chopper descends.
The thut-thut-thut suspends
mid-air. A genie sprinkles
fairy sugar. Whirled into the air.
Falling everywhere.
Each blade of grass,
a frozen confection.
Each spring blossom,
preserved perfection.

The Words Shaking Free

With thanks to Elizabeth Barrett Browning

When my own soul stands up erect, strong,
seventy years sprawling backwards, the future
dawning near and nearer: what bitter wrong
can there be, that I should not gather
more contentment?

Think: From minister's daughter, to wedded wife,
to lesbian life. Through child-raising, dog-training,
bread-baking. Through garden-planting and
tomato-canning. As camp director, pool operator,
music teacher, flute performer.

I have stood before thousands with music in my hands.
I have stood with children clinging to my skirts, and
known it all to be snatched away. I have stood before
doctors, allergists, immunologists, infectious disease
specialists, my body imploding with sickness and grief.

We came to the mountains to heal. My deep, dear silence
is pierced: We Do Not Want Queers in This County.

And I sing the perfect song, spin the silver silky thread
of Debussy, Bach, Ravel, Poulenc. While the beloved
cooks kale and carrots from the garden, I fill the air
with shimmering song. I will stay here, in this remote
cove, where deer graze out my window, chickadees

visit the feeder, wrens nest on the porch. I will
stand up tall and strong. Claim this place to stand
and love in, for today and tomorrow. However many
days are left. With darkness and light. Wind
rattling the trees. The words shaking free.

Chicory

Bachelor button
Bobbing blue
Favorite flower
Dresden hue

Sky blue
Williamsburg Blue
Blue as your eyes
Blue as china

Fleeting as a summer day
I cannot capture it

Cannot put it in a vase
    or it wilts
Cannot pick it
    or it dies
Cannot transplant it
    or it won't take
Not pretty to look at
    if you look it straight

Beautiful only
    if you walk by
Blue blur
Blue blaze
Out of the corner
Of your eye

Radio Culture Collage

Flipping through radio stations
while driving through the South

The third annual BBQ Cook-Off will be held Southern-Style!
Come enjoy the fixins'! Are YOU willing? Have YOU recognized

the sovereignty of God? Summer camp registration can be
accessed on the website. Chance of a thunderstorm continues.

Prayer recognizes God's mercy. But God cannot forgive our sins,
unless WE put away sin, FIRST. Get a Ruger LCRX, .38 Special,

on sale now. 50% off all firearm accessories, 10% off all ammo.
That's the Hunter's Den! Call or stop by today! Up next,

the BBC Concert Orchestra, conducted by Leonard Slatkin.
Bring your taters and lawn chairs! Get discounted tickets!

Brought to you by Mountain Pure Spring Water, committed
to a zero-waste facility! Come to the North Carolina

Sweet Potato Festival. Rain or shine! Bring your glass or plastic
returnable bottles! We're looking at a rather cloudy day today.

Stop in at Hazel's Drive-Thru, for our homemade biscuits
and gravy. The only place on your radio dial, where every song

is guaranteed Real Country. Book now! Final registration!
50% off optics and lasers! Bring the whole family!

Praise Song

Praise for the morning fog creeping up the cove.
Praise for it seeping in the window. Praise
for my wife's warm body lying next to mine,
her damp curls tickling my spine. Praise for
hot coffee, flush toilets. For the thrush
singing my morning devotional as I walk
through wet grass in old boots. Praise for
email friends, phone messages. Praise that
my computer works, joints aren't inflamed,
I am not sick in bed another day. Praise
for every day I am up doing, thinking, creating.
Able to sit, or walk on my own two feet,
and smell the glorious air.

To Coriander

Your black cushion
sits empty.
Usually you sit there, regal,
a sphinx,
protectress of the valley.
Not a bird flies or a leaf falls
without your knowledge.

Your ventures out,
ventures in,
your circles, barks, whines,
your emotional pulls
and bodily needs
frame my days.

Your absence
has left a void
no human can fill,
a silence
beyond loneliness.
You are
the only being
with whom I am safe.
Please   come   home.

Pas de Deux

I dance in circles.
My feet pirouette to
the ¾ beat of a waltz.
Slow, my arms ballet an arc.
Flow Right, two, three,
Left, two, three.
My hair brushes my shoulders.
Skirt caresses my thighs.

You dance with me.
Your black velvet coat
at my fingertips.
We weave through the room.
Sway together.
Your brown eyes
gaze into my blue.

Breathing together,
the crescendo rises
in unison.
Blend of woman and dog.
Connection beyond species.
Pas de deux.
Canine and she wolf.

Coyotes

The night the goat died
thunder rolled a salute
sky opened
weeping rain
screech owl wailed
coyotes came
the yips began
a clamoring caterwaul
echoing off bleak mountains

The next morning
screech owl whinnied
waking me from sound sleep
yips and yaps
the chorus again
coyotes careening
working a crescendo
howling sounds
their doleful chords

I sat up in darkness
cranked open the window
wondered
how they knew
the goat died
those primal hearts
circling the campfire

What Kind of Support Does Your Garden Need?

With thanks to Maile Louise

Super-Sturdy Supports
Invisible Support
Versatile Support
Ladder Supports

Sturdy Support for
Determinate Tomatoes
Half-Round Supports
Cone-Shaped Supports
Most Flexible Supports

Tidy Up Borders
And Pathways
Wherever
Whenever it's Needed

Stunning!
Self-Gripping!
In Four Heights!

Simply Elegant

Inspired by
The Gardens of France

Use Now!

Standing in the Fog

Seven in the morning
On top of the mountain
In the fog   In the pasture
In weeds   Up to my armpits
Waiting for the fencers to arrive

The thrush sings
Millions of insects feast
On my exposed skin

I stand alone   On hundreds of acres
One moment   Shrouded in fog
The next minute   The vapor shifts
Revealing layers   Of mountains
Vast panorama   Steeple in the far distance
White cows   Standing on a grassy knoll
Half a mile away

The undulating vapor   Shifts again
Clarity disappears
The cows and I   Shrouded in pervasive moisture
Alone   In our own cocoons
Just the air   The grass   Our own heartbeats

The air shifts   Vapor clouds disperse
I am pulled   To the miles beyond
Try to memorize   The vision
Hold perspective

Until the moisture   Shifts again
And I am engulfed   In my own situation
A bug in my right ear   Another gnawing my left wrist
Water dripping down   The back of my neck
My hips burn   From standing

There is no chair   Or dry rock
Only vast expanses   Of towering sedge
Goldenrod   Joe-pye weed   Blackberry   Milkweed
Lost in my senses   No matter what   The vapor does
Just as lying safely   In my dry bed   An hour ago

Waves of moisture   Follow the slopes   Up from the valley
I stand   My world changing
The sun rises   My bladder fills
I listen   Watch   Breathe   Wait

Dear Subcontractor
A Rant

In the past, I paid you hourly. I paid you cost-plus.
Whatever the agreement, you were the one
paid to do the work. I purchased the materials.

You waltzed in without tools, without a truck
to get to the site. I fetched the screws,
drivers and bits, plugged and unplugged your cords,

vacuumed sawdust long after you were home
drinking your beer. You made errors. I brainstormed
solutions. I purchased more materials. Paid you hourly

to fix your errors. You always had an excuse. It was
never your fault. Blamed the wood that warped,
the wall that was not plumb, the floor that was not flat,

the worker who worked before you. This time
the job was clear. Build this desk on this spot.
Here are the measurements. But, please measure

for yourself. Still, there are errors. It is never your fault.
You use the same excuse: it is the wood that is warped,
the wall that is not plumb, the floor that is not flat.

Now, you say the outlets are in the wrong place,
the file cabinet is too long, the printer plug too large
for the hole you cut.

I tell you: This floor? This wall? This ceiling? This
outlet? You installed them all, yourself. This file
cabinet and printer plug? They were all here

when you measured for the job. You claim
you are losing money on this project. I am delighted
this time you are working for contract price. I will not

have to pay you hourly to solve the problems. For once,
I get the satisfaction of knowing you are paying
for your own mistakes.

A Stitch in Time

A stitch in time saves nine. A diller a dollar,
a ten o'clock scholar. Waste not want not.
Some like it hot, some like it cold. Some
like it in the pot. Send the needle in, send
the needle out, send the needle round about.

The rain is raining all around, it falls
on field and tree. As you sew, so shall you rip.
Quilt till you wilt. Halfway down is a place I sit.
Quilters know all the angles. But she'll be
coming round the mountain when she comes,

and we'll all go out to meet her, when she comes.
And the fabric of my soul, and the fabric
of your soul, knit together in such a fine tight weave
that Red Rover, Red Rover won't dare come over.
But the Big Bad Wolf will huff and puff,

and the porridge will get cold. The sheep's
in the fold, and Little Miss Muffet still sits
on her tuffet. The needle goes in, the needle
goes out, the worms play pinochle on your snout.
Stitch your stress away. Love is the thread

that binds us. Buttons and patches,
and the cold wind blowing, the days pass quickly
when I am sewing. Miss Lydia Banks
is never rude. Annabelle Lee lives by the sea.
Old Man River, just sitting there with

Hickory Dickory Dock. I don't want to
sew a frock. I'd rather quilt around the clock.
While Ding Dong Dell, Pussy's in the well.
Who put her there? I have no idea.
But I keep my end-tables full of quilts,

so I don't have to dust them. All my
scattered moments are taken up
with my needle. If I stitch fast enough,
does it count as aerobic exercise?
And the Queen of Hearts made some tarts,

the Knave came and took away. And
what'll you do with the baby-o
if he won't go to sleepy-o? Wrap him up
in calico, and send him to his mammy-o.
When life throws you scraps, just make a quilt.

I am a Material Girl. Do you wanna see
my fabric collection? A quilt will warm your body,
comfort your soul. I hem my blessings with
thankfulness. My work is stitched with love.
But silver thread and golden needles

cannot mend this heart of mine. When I have
a thread and needle, I sew a crazy quilt. A line
might take hours, never a second's thought.
Quilters never grow old, we just go to pieces.
Sewing mends the marrow, something to show

for all the effort. Wanted: a needle swift enough
to stitch this country back together. To achieve
that kind of work, is really some delicate stitching.
In this crazy quilt of life, I am glad you're in
my block of friends.

Hot July

Hum of insects
Biting, buzzing, chirping
Black-eyed Susans
Bachelor buttons
Daisies
Lizard idles on a rock

Beads of sweat
Trickle down
Sticky skin
Damp underwear
Frizzed hair
Unquenchable thirst

Too hot for the birds
Too hot for work
Flowers wilt
Cats laze on the stoop
I sit on the porch
Drink iced tea

Afternoon thunderstorm
Dinner not soon enough
A cool shower
Whispered breeze
Evening returns
Down the mountain

The Moth

Into the steamy outdoor shower,
shrouded in the dark fog
of early morning,
flew a moth
large as my hand.

It flustered towards
and around the light,
succumbing to the shimmering
iridescent luminescence.
I could almost feel its gravitational pull,
the razor's edge of delight yielding
to my huge halogen.

Standing there mutely, naked,
I could see it seem to
summon all its strength,
trying to leave.

As gracefully as it fluttered in,
it most ungracefully tried to flutter out.
Flopping around,
crashing into the wall,
careening into me,
getting caught in my towel,
almost drowning in the stream of hot water.

I tried, of course, to help it,
but there was nothing to do
but watch.
So blinded and crazed,
trying to survive,
while being pulled incessantly
towards light.
Towards death.

Meditation

Go into the dark   Shut your eyes
Go deep into yourself   Swallow long
Slow   Feel your soul shudder   Settle in
To your own breath   In the deep quiet

Of the night   In the deep quiet
Of early morning   Before the fog
Before the dew   Under the stars
Under the moon   Let your arms surround

Your own   Soft shoulders   Inspire your own
Sacred space   Go into the dark   Go into
The sadness   Let the tears come   The despair
The yearning   Embrace the bleak blackness

Of your hunger   Suckle the sustenance   Of silence
Go into the dark   Leave the light behind   The pain
The worries   The drain of consciousness   Surrender
Your intellect   Embrace the longing   Go into the dark

Partake the drowsy morsels   The damp dewy
Moments of solitude   Nurse the memories
Of enchanted emptiness

Homecoming

Soon you will be here
Porch light is on
Crickets chirp impatience
Katydid   Katydidn't
Screech owl whinnies

I set a clean placemat   For you
Brush my hair   Button my shirt
In our room   Clean sheets await
Sound of tires   On gravel
You coming up   The drive

The silence of the cove   Recedes

The Grandmother Tree Fell

Winter had been harsh. For days the snow fell. Layers of encrusted melt hardened in the freeze. Mid-February, the immense tree quivered. The thud shook the house. Ground heaved next to her heavy footprint. Rumble reverberated. I have heard that all trees are interconnected. Underground, they transfer warnings, information, nutrients. With communal interdependence, they dispatch hormonal and electrical signals through a mycorrhizal network, that, when severed, resembles the wounding of human tissue. When the grandmother tree fell, this bridge was cut. The bonds severed. Upbraided, she lay alone on enameled snow. Her roots jagged and ripped. Later, the turbulence calmed. Discordant pandemonium quieted. Anarchy stilled. The cats went back to sleep. Birds returned to the feeder.

Yellow

It lay on the ground, dead. The sharp-shinned hawk.
Belly-up on the lawn. Yellow feet, plastic.
The last crayon in the box. Paper wrapper of skin
peeled back. Eyes frozen in place, still tracking its prey.

That afternoon, the cats left a weasel belly-up
on the stoop. Punctured in the abdomen,
a squiggle-worm of intestine protruded yellow.

Later, we walked the logging road up the mountain.
At the top, breathless, we turned, glanced back.
Our house in the distance, sheltered in the golden folds
of Fork Mountain. Butter yellow in the setting sun.

White Cows on a Green Hill

Leave town behind. Turn right at Glen Raven Mills, there where United Community Bank is on the corner. Drive up past Lotawatah Road, past Heritage Baptist Church, up the hill past the house with the four rounded-over trees, past Roland's house. Roland who died last year, where the family of renters now live. Pass Debbie's mother's house. Debbie's mother who died last year. Come on round the curve, steeply downhill, make the sharp turn to the left. Pass the house with the Electrolux sign,

pass Moonshine Mountain, Clearmont Fire Department, Mine Fork Free Will Baptist Church, Old Mine Fork Road. Keep on driving downhill, pass the sign for Green Mountain Township. Come on around the corner. Echo Hill Lane with the kudzu growing on the right. Pass Upper Pig Pen Road, Lower Pig Pen Road. Pass the house with the Halloween decorations and Christmas lights year-round. Better slow down to twenty-five miles an hour before the sharp right-hand curve,

or you won't make it. The river is now on your left. Careful of wet spots on the road that freeze in winter. Pass Sugar Creek Road, Unimin Mine. Pass the swinging bridge connecting houses to the other side. Come through Brushy Creek Township, past Double Island Road. Then you hit the flat where there are no houses, no signs. Only the river on one side, dark forest on the other. No passing, no one. Nothing until the new bridge. Then the railroad. The house with the dogs tied up. House with the mule.

Red Hill Recycling Center, Red Hill Beauty Salon. Pass Red Hill Hardware that was abandoned three years ago, but still has the "Come On In, We're Open" sign hanging on the door. When you get to the white house with the white cows, on the green hill, you are close to our place. When you get to the white house, on the green hill, with the white cows, all the cows grazing in the same direction, working their way across the green hill, you will see the man tending his land and his cows. The man who mows

and moves fresh hay. The man who works on his red barn, walks in his red boots, mends his fence. Everything is tended, everything is fine. The world is okay. Drive on past the white cows. Pass the new guardrails where the road caved in during the gully-washer last autumn. Pass the barn that fell over last winter, the house with the bank iris, Harrell Hill Road. Everything is overgrown, joe-pye weed hangs over the road. Driveways are washed out from summer rains, mildew on the porches,

laundry still damp on the line. Drive on past Friendship Chapel, The Ridges of Rock Creek, Bad Creek, Mulberry Lane. Pass the house with the unfinished solar panels, past where we saw the bear cross the road last spring. Continue to Pine Root Road. Turn right. Come on up the road, just a short way. You have arrived at our home. The mail is still in the box. Weeds hang over the driveway. Road bars are full of silt. Garden is going to seed. Cats are hungry. Wood sits needing to be split.

When I drive up our driveway, I think of his cows. I think of the white cows on the green hill. The man tending his cows. I think of his grass that is tended, not perfect, just tended. And I remember everything is fine. Just fine.

Drinking Tea

Breakfast on the sun porch
Warm muffins and butter
Spirals of steam
Curl up from my tea

I wrote those lines
When I was thirty
Celebrating my birthday
Thinking my tea
Was ready to drink

Now at seventy
I am only recently learning
To sleep in my chair by the fire
Chin nodding onto chest
Book in position
Frozen in time

Time moves on
Gray hairs
Creased lines
I am only now
Realizing how
Much is asked
Of one who wants
To drink tea

October Full Moon

Standing on the hill, I look down the cove.
The roof glows radiant in the moonlight. It is
so bright, tonight I can see this page, clearly.

Stars canopy above. A chill in the air.
Dark forest forms a fringe to the scent
of rotting leaves, decaying grass. Last remaining
katydids sing their fading ostinato. Air is
electric with light, life at its zenith.

Inside my fleece jacket, I am warm. My blood
pulsates the liquid music of my life. Alive
in my veins. Electric.

When I am too old to stand here any longer,
will I wish I had stood here more?

About the Author

Marilyn McVicker had her first poem published in 1980, and has been writing ever since.

Her poetry has appeared in *Kakalak*, *Kaleidoscope*, *The Healing Muse*, *Earth's Daughters*, *Speckled Trout Review*, *Wordgathering*, and other journals.

Her published books include:
As for Life: A memoir in poetry exploring the isolation & loss of chronic illness (Redhawk Publications, 2022),
Some Shimmer of You (Finishing Line Press, 2014), and
Sauna Detoxification Therapy (McFarland & Co., Inc., 1997).

Marilyn's fascination with words and self-expression stems from her previous career as a solo flutist and music educator, and her family experience with deaf culture.

All photos for this book were taken in Long Field Hollow.
www.marilynmcvicker.org

www.ingramcontent.com/pod-product-compliance
Ingram Content Group UK Ltd.
Pitfield, Milton Keynes, MK11 3LW, UK
UKHW062308290726
14090UKWH00018B/942